BERKSHIRE
Wit & Humour

Clyde from
Peg & Clare

LILLY LODDON

BRADWELL
BOOKS

Published by Bradwell Books
9 Orgreave Close Sheffield S13 9NP
Email: books@bradwellbooks.co.uk
Compiled by Lilly Loddon

All rights reserved. No part of this publication may be reproduced, stored in a retrieval system or transmitted in any form or by any means, electronic, mechanical, photocopying, recording or otherwise without the prior permission of Bradwell Books.

British Library Cataloguing in Publication Data: a catalogue record for this book is available from the British Library.

1st Edition

ISBN: 9781909914636

Print: Gomer Press, Llandysul, Ceredigion SA44 4JL
Design by: jenksdesign@yahoo.co.uk/07506 471162
Illustrations: ©Tim O'Brien 2014

A couple from the Tilehurst had been courting for nearly twenty years. One day as they sat on a seat in the park, the woman plucked up the courage to ask, "Don't you think it's time we got married?" Her sweetheart answered, "Yes, but who'd have us?"

A teacher at a school in Bracknell was having a little trouble getting her Year 11 pupils to understand grammar. "These are what we call the pronouns," she said, "We use them with verbs like this: I am, you are, he/she is." The pupils looked at her with glazed expressions.

Trying a different tack, she said, "Lauren, give me a sentence with the pronoun, 'I' in it."

Lauren began, "I is..." "No, no, no, no, no NO, NO!" shouted the teacher, "Never, 'I is', always, 'I am'... now try again."

Lauren looked puzzled and a little hurt, thought a while then began again more quietly, "I... am...the ninth letter of the alphabet."

BERKSHIRE Wit & Humour

Simon was down on his luck so he thought he would try getting a few odd jobs by calling at the posh houses in Bray Lock. After a few "no ways", a guy in one of the big houses thought he would give him a break and says, "The porch needs painting so I'll give you £50 to paint it for me."

"You're life-saver, mister," says Simon, "I'll get started right away!" Time passes until…

"There you go, I'm all done with the painting."

"Well, here's your £50," says the homeowner, handing over some crisp tenners.
"Thanks very much," says Simon, pocketing the money, "Oh and by the way, it's a Ferrari, not a Porsche!"

BERKSHIRE Wit & Humour

Two rival cricketers from Bucklebury and Bradfield were having a chat.

"The local team wants me to play for them very badly," said the man from Bucklebury.

"Well," said his friend, "You're just the man for the job."

Insurance Assessor: "What gear were you in at the moment of the impact?"

Woman Driver: "Gucci sweats and Reeboks."

Two elderly ladies were enjoying a small sherry at home in Cookham. One said to the other, "Was it love at first sight when you met your late husband?"

"No, I don't think so," came the reply, "I didn't know how much money he had when I first met him!"

A rather cocky young man, who worked on a busy construction site in Slough, was bragging that he could outdo anyone in a feat of strength. He made a special case of making fun of Morris, one of the more senior workmen. After several minutes, Morris had had enough.

"Why don't you put your money where your mouth is?" he said. "I'll bet a week's wages that I can haul something in a wheelbarrow over to that outbuilding that you won't be able to wheel back again."

"You're on, mate," the over-confident young man replied. "It's a bet! Let's see what you got."

Morris reached out and grabbed the wheelbarrow by the handles. Then, nodding to the young man, he said, "All right. Get in."

BERKSHIRE Wit & Humour

A lawyer from Chalfont St. Giles and a businessman from Windsor ended up sitting next to each other on a long-haul flight.

The lawyer started thinking that he could have some fun at the man from Windsor's expense and asked him if he'd like to play a fun game. The businessman was tired and just wanted to relax. He politely declined the offer and tried to sleep. The lawyer persisted, explaining, "I ask you a question, and if you don't know the answer, you pay me just £5; you ask me one, and if I don't know the answer, I will pay you £500."

This got the businessman a little more interested and he finally agreed to play the game.

The lawyer asked the first question, "What's the distance from the Earth to the moon?"

The man from Windsor said nothing, but reached into his pocket, pulled out a five-pound note and handed it to the lawyer.

Now, it was his turn to ask a question. He asked the lawyer, "What goes up a hill with three legs, and comes down with four?"

The lawyer scratched his head. He looked the question up on his laptop and searched the web. He sent emails to his most well-read friends. He used the air-phone to call his colleagues in Chalfont St. Giles, but he still came up with nothing. After over an hour of searching, he finally gave up. He woke up the businessman and handed him £500. The man pocketed the cash smugly and dozed off again.

The lawyer was wild with curiosity and wanted to know the answer. He shook the businessman awake. "Well? What goes up a hill with three legs and comes down with four?" he demanded.

The businessman reached into his pocket, handed the lawyer £5 and went straight back to sleep.

BERKSHIRE Wit & Humour

A man from Reading said to his wife, "Get your coat on love. I'm off to the club".

His wife said, "That's nice. You haven't taken me out for years".
He said, "You're not coming with me...I'm turning the heating off when I go out".

A well-known academic from Buckinghamshire New University was giving a lecture on the philosophy of language at Reading University. He came to a curious aspect of English grammar.

"You will note," said the somewhat stuffy scholar, "That in the English language, two negatives can mean a positive, but it is never the case that two positives can mean a negative."

To which someone at the back responded, "Yeah, yeah."

A bloke from Newbury goes into an artist's studio and asks if the artist could paint a picture of him surrounded by beautiful, scantily clad women. The artist agrees but he is intrigued by this strange request. He asks his new client why he wants such a picture painted and the bloke says, "Well, if I die before me missus when she finds this painting she'll wonder which one I spent all me money on!"

The next day the bloke's wife goes into the artist's studio and asks him to paint her wearing a big diamond necklace and matching earrings.

"Of course, madam," says the artist, "but may I ask why?"

"Well," replies the woman, "if I die before me husband I want his new woman to be frantic searching for all me jewellery!"

BERKSHIRE Wit & Humour

Derek and Duncan were long-time neighbours in Sandhurst. Every time, Derek saw Duncan coming round to his house, his heart sank. This was because he knew that, as always, Duncan would be visiting him in order to borrow something and he was fed up with it.

"I'm not going to let Duncan get away with it this time," he said quietly to his wife, "Watch what I'm about to do."

"Hi there, I wondered if you were thinking about using your hedge trimmer this afternoon?" asked Duncan.

"Oh, I'm very sorry," said Derek, trying to look apologetic, "but I'm actually going to be using it all afternoon."

"In that case," replied Duncan with a big grin, "You won't be using your golf clubs, will you? Mind if I borrow them?"

A young banker from Ascot decided to get his first tailor-made suit. As he tried it on, he reached down to put his hands in the pockets but to his surprise found none.

He mentioned this to the tailor who asked him, "You're a banker, right?" The young man answered, "Yes, I am."

"Well, whoever heard of a banker put his hand in his own pocket?"

Two aerials meet on a roof, fall in love, get married. The ceremony was rubbish - but the reception was brilliant.

A housewife went to the greengrocer's in Aldermarston. She picked up a lettuce and examined it. "Why is it that these iceberg lettuces just seem to be getting smaller and smaller?" she asked the shop assistant.

"Global warming," he replied.

Builder: "I've been putting roofs on houses in a village in Berkshire."

His mate: "Thatcham?"

Builder: "No, slates."

A Berkshire man is driving through Buckinghamshire, when he passes a farmer standing in the middle of a huge field. He pulls the car over and watches the farmer standing stock-still, doing absolutely nothing. Intrigued, the man walks over to the farmer and asks him, "Excuse me sir, but what are you doing?" The farmer replies, "I'm trying to win a Nobel Prize."

"How?" Asks the puzzled Berkshire man.

"Well," says the farmer, "I heard they give the prize to people who are outstanding in their field."

BERKSHIRE Wit & Humour

A police officer was patrolling the lanes outside Wokingham one night, when he noticed a car swerving all over the road. Quickly, he turned on his lights and siren and pulled the driver over. "Sir, do you know you're all over the road? Please step out of the car."

When the man got out of the car, the policeman told him to walk in a straight line.

"I'd be happy to, offisher," said the drunk, "If you can just get the line to stop moving about."

At a large house in Theale, the doorbell rings. The lady of the house answers the front door to find a man with a toolbox standing on her porch.

"May I help you?" she asks.

"I'm the piano tuner." he says.

"But I didn't send for a piano tuner.' she exclaims.

"No," he replies. "Your neighbors did."

Resolving to surprise her husband, an investment banker's wife from Remenham pops by his office in the City. She finds him with his secretary sitting in his lap. Without hesitation, he starts dictating, "...and in conclusion, gentlemen, credit crunch or no credit crunch, I cannot continue to operate this office with just one chair!"

Man: "How do I start a small business?"

Bank manager: "Start a large one and wait six months."

What do you call the two people that always have to embarrass you the most in front of all your friends?
Mum and Dad.

At a cricket match in Newbury, a fast bowler sent one down and it just clipped the bail. As nobody yelled "Ow's att", the batsman picked up the bail and replaced it. He looked at the umpire and said, "Windy today isn't it?"

"Yes," said the umpire, "Mind it doesn't blow your cap off when you're walking back to the pavilion."

Sherlock Holmes and Dr. Watson are camping on Walbury Hill, contemplating a new mystery. After a good meal and a bottle of wine, they lay down for the night, and went to sleep. Some hours later, Holmes awoke and nudged his faithful friend. "Watson, look up at the sky and tell me what you see."

Watson looked up and replied, "I see millions and millions of stars."

"What does that tell you?" asked Holmes.
Watson pondered for a minute. "Astronomically, it tells me that there aremillions of galaxies, and potentially billions of planets. Astrologically, I observe that Saturn is in Leo. Horologically, I deduce that the time is approximately a quarter past three. Meteorologically, I suspect that we will have a beautiful day tomorrow. What does it tell you, Sherlock?"

Holmes was silent for a minute, then spoke. "It tells me that someone has stolen our tent."

An elderly couple from Hungerford are sitting at the dining table in their semi-detached house talking about making preparations for writing their wills. Bill says to his missus, Edna, "I've been thinking, my dear, if I go first to meet me maker I don't want you to be on your own for too long. In fact, I think you could do worse than marry Colin in the Chemists or Dave with the fruit stall in the market. They'd provide for you and look after you when I'm gone."

"That's very kind on you to think about me like that, Bill," replied Edna, "But I've already made my own arrangements!"

Miss Malaprop was telling a colleague about the wonderful evening she had had the night before at the Sadlers Wells ballet up in town. She commented on the wonderful costumes, the fantastic orchestra and, most of all, on how graceful the dancers were, "They just slid across that stage like they were on casternets!"

A policeman stops a drunk wandering the streets of Slough at four in the morning and says, "Can you explain why you are out at this hour, sir?"

The drunk replies, "If I was able to explain myself, I would have been home with the wife ages ago."

A reporter from the Slough Observer was covering the local football league match between Slough Town and Maidenhead United F.C. One of the Slough Town players looked so old he went over to him and said, "You know you might be the oldest man playing in the league. How do you do it at your age?"

The man replied, "I drink six pints of larger every night, smoke two packets of fags a day, and eat loads of kebabs."

"Wow, that is incredible!" said the reporter, "How old did you say you were?"

"Twenty-two," said the player proudly.

A Maidenhead couple, Enid and Sidney, are having matrimonial difficulties and seek the advice of a counsellor. The couple are shown into a room where the counsellor asks Enid what problems, in her opinion, she faces in her relationship with Sidney.

"Well," she starts, "he shows me no affection, I don't seem to be important to him anymore. We don't share the same interests and I don't think he loves me at all." Enid has tears in her eyes as the counsellor walks over to her, gives her a big hug and kisses her firmly on the lips.

Sidney looks on in passive disbelief. The counsellor turns to Sidney and says, "This is what Enid needs once a day for the next month. Can you see that she gets it?"

Sidney looks unsettled, "Well I can drop her off everyday other than Wednesdays when I play snooker and Sundays when I go fishing!"

A man from Bucks went into a hardware store and asked to buy a sink.

"Would you like one with a plug?" asked the assistant.
"Don't tell me they've gone electric now!" said the man.

What do you get if you cross Milton Keynes Dons with an OXO cube?
A laughing stock.

A young couple were pulling up at their honeymoon hotel in Windsor. The new bride felt very self-conscious about the fact that she was a newly-wed. She turned to her new husband and asked, "What can we do to hide the fact that we are on our honeymoon?"

The young man thought for a second then replied, "I know - you can carry the luggage!"

Did you hear about the magic tractor? It drove up the lane and turned into a field.

Just before the Ascot Gold Cup, the trainer was giving last minute instructions to the jockey and appeared to slip something into the horse's mouth just as a steward walked by. "What was that?" inquired the steward.

"Oh nothing," said the trainer, "just a mint."

He offered one to the steward and had one himself. After the suspicious steward had left the scene, the trainer continued with his instructions.

"Just keep on the rail. You're on a dead cert. The only thing that could possibly pass you down the home straight is either the steward or me."

BERKSHIRE Wit & Humour

A man went to the doctor one day and said, "I've just been playing rugby for the Newbury Blues and when I got back, I found that when I touched my legs, my arms, my head and everywhere else, it really hurt."

After a thorough examination the doctor said, "You've broken your finger."

A woman got on a bus in Bracknell but soon regretted it. The driver sped down the high street, zigzagging across the lanes, breaking nearly every rule of the road. Unable to take it any longer, the woman stepped forward, her voice shaking as she spoke. "You're a shocking driver! I am so afraid of sitting on your bus, I don't know what to do."

"Do what I do," said the bus driver. "Close your eyes!"

At The Woodpecker pub in Wash Water, a newcomer asked a local man, "Have you lived here all your life?"

The old man took a sip of his bitter and, after a long pause, replied, "Don't know yet!"

A labourer in Reading, shouted up to his roofer mate on top of an old terraced house, saying, "Don't start climbing down this ladder, Bert."

"Why not?" Bert called back.

"Cos I moved it five minutes ago!" replied his mate.

A police officer arrived at the scene of a major pile up on the M4.

The officer runs over to the front car and asks the driver, "Are you seriously hurt?"

The driver turns to the officer and says, "How the heck should I know? Do I look like a lawyer?"

A pupil at a school in Bracknell asked his teacher, "Are 'trousers' singular or plural?"

The teacher replied, "They're singular on top and plural on the bottom."

A bloke walked up to the foreman of a road laying gang in Slough and asked for a job. "I haven't got one for you today," said the foreman, looking up from his newspaper. "But if you walk half a mile down there, you'll find the gang and you can see if you like the work. I can put you on the list for tomorrow." "That's great, mate," said the bloke as he wandered off down the road.

At the end of the shift, the man walked past the foreman and shouted, "Thanks, mate. See you in the morning."
The foreman looked up from his paper and called back, "You've enjoyed yourself then?"

"Yes, I have!" the bloke shouted, "But can I have a shovel or a pick to lean on like the rest of the gang tomorrow?"

BERKSHIRE Wit & Humour

Sam worked in a telephone marketing company in Twyford. One day he walked into his boss's office and said, "I'll be honest with you, I know the economy isn't great, but I have three companies after me, and, with respect, I would like to ask for a pay rise."

After a few minutes of haggling, his manager finally agreed to a 5% pay rise, and Sam happily got up to leave.

"By the way," asked the boss as Sam went to the door, "which three companies are after you?"

"The electric company, the water company, and the phone company," Sam replied.

BERKSHIRE Wit & Humour

A farmer was driving along a country road near the village of Midgham Green with a large load of fertiliser. A little boy, playing in front of his house, saw him and called out, "What do you have on your truck?"

"Fertiliser," the farmer replied.

"What are you going to do with it?" asked the little boy.

"Put it on strawberries," answered the farmer.

"You ought to live here," the little boy advised him. "We put sugar and cream on ours."

BERKSHIRE Wit & Humour

Outside the Madejski stadium, two London Irish rugby fans were talking…

First fan: "I wish I'd brought the piano to the stadium."

Second fan: "Why would you bring a piano to the football game?"

First fan: "Because I left the tickets on it."

A young couple from Windsor were doing some shopping in Reading. Having purchased everything they needed, they returned to the car park to drive home.

"Where's the car?" said the wife. "Someone's stolen it!"

They went off to the local police station and reported the theft.

Miserably, the couple walked back towards the train station but as they passed the car park, there was their stolen car, back in the exact same spot! On the windshield, there was an envelope with a note inside which read:

Please accept my apologies for borrowing your car but my wife went into labour and I had to get her to the maternity hospital.

I am now the proud father of a baby boy. Please accept the two tickets enclosed for the musical at the Novello Theatre tonight as a mark of my gratitude. Thanks.

The young couple's faith in humanity was restored and they went off to Ascot to the show and had a wonderful time.

They arrive home to Windsor late that night to find that they'd been burgled and the entire contents of their house had been taken. On the front door was a note, which read, *Sorry, but we have to put the kid through university one day.*

The president of the Windsor Vegetarian Society really couldn't control himself any more. He simply had to try some pork, just to see what it tasted like. So one day he told his members he was going away for a short break. He left town and headed to a restaurant in Eton. He sat down, ordered a roasted pig, and waited impatiently for his treat. After only a few minutes, he heard someone call his name, and, to his horror, he saw one of his members walking towards him. At exactly the same moment, the waiter arrived at his table, with a huge platter, holding a whole roasted pig with an apple in its mouth. "Isn't this place something?" said the president, thinking quickly, "Look at the way they serve apples!"

One freezing cold December day, two blondes went for a walk through Swinley Forest in search of the perfect Christmas tree. Finally, after five hours looking, one turns to the other and says crossly, "That's it, I've had enough. I'm chopping down the next fir tree we see, whether it's decorated or not!"

Phil's nephew came to him with a problem. "I have my choice of two women," he said, with a worried frown, "A beautiful, penniless young girl whom I love dearly, and a rich widow who I don't really love."

"Follow your heart," Phil counselled, "marry the girl you love."

"Very well, Uncle Phil," said the nephew, "That's sound advice. Thank you."

"You're welcome," replied Phil with a smile, "By the way, where does the widow live?"

Two Theale and Tilehurst Cricket Club players are chatting in the bar after a match. "So did you have a hard time explaining last week's game to the wife?" says one.

"I certainly did," says the other, "She found out I wasn't there!"

Riding the favourite in the Lockinge Stakes at Newbury, the jockey is well ahead of the field. Suddenly he's hit on the head by a free-range turkey and a string of sausages. He manages to keep control of his mount and pulls back into the lead, only to be struck by a box of Christmas crackers and a dozen mince pies as he goes over the last fence. With great skill he manages to steer the horse to the front of the field once more then, on the home straight, he's struck on the head by a bottle of sherry and a Christmas pudding. Thus distracted, he comes in second. He immediately goes to the stewards to complain that he has been seriously hampered.

A passenger in a taxi tapped the driver on the shoulder to ask him something.

The driver screamed, lost control of the cab, nearly hit a bus, drove up over the curb and stopped just inches from a large plate glass window.

For a few moments everything was silent in the cab, then the driver said, "Please, don't ever do that again. You scared the daylights out of me."

The passenger, who was also frightened, apologised and said he didn't realise that a tap on the shoulder could frighten him so much, to which the driver replied, "I'm sorry, it's really not your fault at all. Today is my first day driving a cab. I've been driving a hearse for the last twenty-five years."

BERKSHIRE Wit & Humour

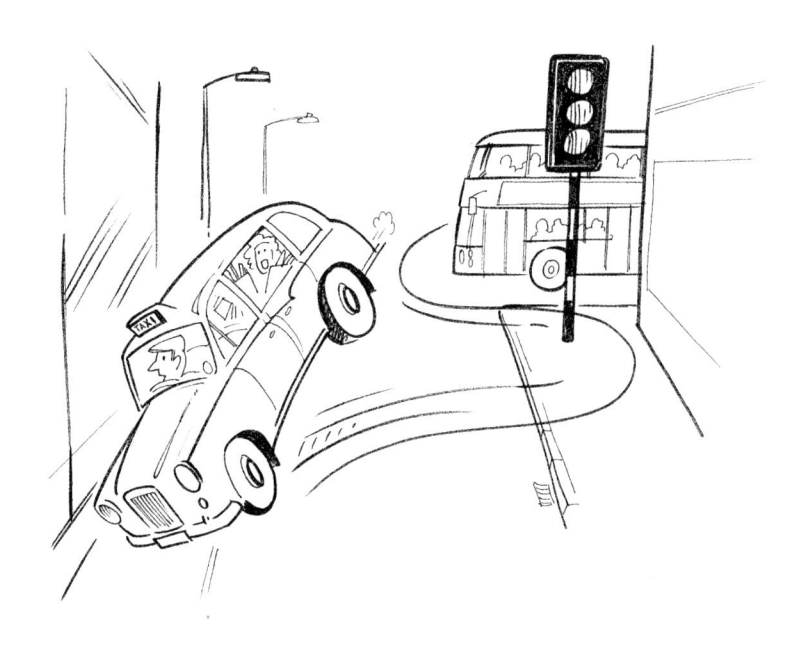

In the early days of television sets the ritual of switching the TV on and waiting for the valves to warm up was all part of building the excitement to watch a programme: usually the one that was on! In Hamstead Marshall an old farmer, Jimmy Woodhead decided to tell his neighbour about his newly-acquired television and how he was going to watch the Queen's Coronation. "I've gotta go in now an' watch the spectacle," he said, looking at his pocket watch.

His neighbour looked and said, "But it ain't on for another three hours."

"I know," said Jimmy, "but they're sayin' there'll be a lot there and I wants to get a good seat!"

An expectant father rang the Wexham Park Maternity Unit to see how his wife, who had gone into labour, was getting on. By mistake, he was connected to the county cricket ground.

"How's it going?" he asked.

"Fine," came the answer, "We've got three out and hope to have the rest out before lunch. The last one was a duck."

Supporters, waiting to watch Slough Town play The Dons, heard that the Dons were going to be delayed.

They saw a sign on the M4 that said "Clean Lavatories"... so they did.

Many years ago there was a dispute between two villages, one in Berkshire and the other in Buckinghamshire. One day the villagers heard the cry, "One man from Berkshire is stronger than one hundred Buckinghamshire men."

The villagers in Buckinghamshire were furious and immediately sent their hundred strongest men to engage with the enemy. They listened, horrified by the screams and shouts. After hours of fighting, all was quiet but none of the men returned.

Later on, the same voice shouted out, "Is that the best you can do?"

This fired up the people from Buckinghamshire and they rallied round, getting a thousand men to do battle. After days of the most frightful blood-curdling sounds, one man emerged from the battlefield, barely able to speak, but with his last breath he managed to murmur, "It's a trap, there's two of them!"

An estate agent parks his beautifully restored E-type Jag in front of the office in Bedford to show it off to his colleagues. As he's getting out of the car, a truck comes along, takes off the door and the driver carries on oblivious to the damage he has caused.

More than a little distraught, the estate agent grabs his mobile and calls the police. Five minutes later, the police arrive. Before the policeman has a chance to ask any questions, the estate agent starts screaming hysterically:

"My Jag, my beautiful beautiful Jag is ruined, it'll simply never be the same again!"

After the estate agent finally finishes his rant, the policeman shakes his head in disgust, "I can't believe how materialistic you estate agents are. You lot are so focused on your possessions that you don't notice anything else in your life."

"How can you say such a thing at a time like this?" snaps the estate agent.

The policeman replies, "Didn't you realise that your right arm was torn off when the truck hit you?"

The estate agent looks down in absolute horror…

"Oh my goodness!" he screams, "Where's my Rolex?!"

Darren proudly drove his new convertible into Windsor and parked it on the main street. He was on his way to the recycling centre to get rid of an unwanted gift, a foot spa, which he left on the back seat.

He had walked half way down the street when he realised that he had left the top down with the foot spa still in the back.

He ran all the way back to his car, but it was too late...another five foot spas had been dumped in the car.

The nervous young batsman playing for Mortimer West End Cricket Club was having a very bad day. In a quiet moment in the game, he muttered to the one of his team mates, "Well, I suppose you've seen worse players."

There was no response...so he said it again, "I said 'I guess you've seen worse players'."

His team mate looked at him and answered, "I heard you the first time. I was just trying to think..."

Slough Town beat The Dons five – nothing; they were lucky to get nothing.

BERKSHIRE Wit & Humour

A farmer from Buckinghamshire once visited a farmer based near Newbury. The visitor asked, "How big is your farm?" to which the Berkshire farmer replied, "Can you see those trees over there? That's the boundary of my farmland".

"Is that all?" said the Buckinghamshire farmer, "It takes me three days to drive to the boundary of my farm."

The Newbury man looked at him and said, "I had a car like that once."

A man from Lambourn bought two horses, but soon realised that he couldn't tell them apart. So he asked the farmer, who lived next door, what he should do. The farmer suggested measuring them. The man came back triumphantly and said, "The white horse is two inches taller than the black horse!"

"I can't believe it," said the American tourist, looking at the grey skies over Windsor Great Park, "I've been here an entire week and it's done nothing but rain. When do you guys get summer over here?"

"Well, that be hard to say, mate." replied the elderly local. "Last year, it was on a Wednesday."

Did you hear about the last wish of the henpecked husband of a house-proud wife?

He asked to have his ashes scattered on the carpet.

A woman from Lambourn called Linda was still not married at thirty-five and she was getting really tired of going to family weddings especially because her old Aunt Maud always came over and said, "You're next!"

It made Linda so annoyed, she racked her brains to figure out how to get Aunt Maud to stop.

Sadly, an old uncle died and there was a big family funeral. Linda spotted Aunt Maud in the crematorium, walked over, pointed at the coffin and said, with a big smile, "You're next!"

At a school in Slough, the maths teacher poses a question to little Josh, "If I give £500 to your dad on 12% interest per annum, what will I get back after two years."

"Nothing," says Josh.

"I am afraid you know nothing about maths, Josh," says the teacher crossly.

"I am afraid too, sir," replies Josh, "you know nothing about my father."

Did you hear about the fight in the chip shop last week? Six fish got battered!

Anne and Matt, a local couple, went to the Berkshire County Fair and found a weighing scale that tells your fortune and weight.

"Hey, listen to this," said Matt, showing his wife a small white card. "It says I'm bright, energetic, and a great husband."

"Yeah," said Anna, "it has your weight wrong as well."

A lawyer at Reading Crown Court says to the judge, "Your Honour, I wish to appeal my client's case on the basis of newly discovered evidence."

His Lordship replies, "And what is the nature of the new evidence?"

The lawyer says, "My Lord, I discovered that my client still has £500 left."

There were two fish in a tank, one says, "You man the guns, I'll drive."

A man and his wife walked past a swanky new restaurant in Windsor. "Did you smell that food?" the woman asked. "Wonderful!"

Being the kind-hearted, generous man that he was, her husband thought, "What the heck, I'll treat her!"

So they walked past it a second time.

One day at Royal Berkshire Hospital, a group of primary school children were being given a tour. A nurse showed them the x-ray machines and asked them if they had ever had broke a bone.

One little boy raised his hand, "I did!"

"Did it hurt?" the nurse asked.

"No!" he replied.

"Wow, you must be a very brave boy!" said the nurse. "What did you break?"

"My sister's arm!"

A man rushed into Royal Berkshire Hospital and asked a nurse for a cure for hiccups. Grabbing a cup of water, the nurse quickly splashed it into the man's face.

"What did you that for?" screamed the man, wiping his face.
"Well, you don't have the hiccups now, do you?" said the nurse.
"No," replied the man. "But my wife out in the car does."

Q: Five estate agents were buried up to their necks in sand – how do you resolve the problem?
A: More sand.

A Hurrah Henry from Buckinghamshire was driving around Newbury in his fancy new car and realised that he was lost. The driver stopped a local character, old Tom, and said, "Hey, you there! Old man, what happens if I turn left here?"

"Don't know sir," replied Tom.

"Well, what if I turn right here - where will that take me?" continued the visitor.

"Don't know, sir," replied old Tom.

Becoming exasperated, the driver continued, "Well, what if I go straight on?"

A flicker of knowledge passed over old Tom's face but then he replied, "Don't know, sir."

"I say old man you don't know a lot do you?" retorted the posh bloke.

Old Tom looked at him and said, "I may not know a lot, sir, but I ain't lost like what you are!" With that, old Tom walked off leaving the motorist stranded.

Two elderly ladies in Greenham had been friends for many decades. Over the years, they had shared all kinds of fun but of late their activities had been limited to meeting a few times a week to play cards. One day, they were playing pontoon when one looked at the other and said, "Now don't get mad at me, dear. I know we've been friends for a long time but I just can't think of your name. I've thought and thought, but I can't remember it. Please tell me what your name is." Her friend got a bit grumpy and, for at least three minutes, she just stared and glared at her. Finally she said, "How soon do you need to know?"